Best Practices
of
Distinguished Schools

Best Practices

of

Distinguished Schools

Thomas Benson

Wisdom House Books

Best Practices of Distinguished Schools

Published by Wisdom House Books, Inc.
Chapel Hill, North Carolina 27517 USA
www.wisdomhousebooks.com

Wisdom House Books is committed to excellence in the publishing industry.

Book design copyright © 2022 by Wisdom House Books, Inc. All rights reserved.

Cover and Interior Design by Ted Ruybal

Published in the United States of America

Paperback ISBN: 979-8-218-04258-5
LCCN: 2022913926

1. EDU034000 | EDUCATION / Educational Policy & Reform / General

2. BUS024000 | BUSINESS & ECONOMICS / Education

3. REF000000 | REFERENCE / General

First Edition

25 24 23 22 21 20 / 10 9 8 7 6 5 4 3 2 1

This Book is dedicated to Dr. Carol Higy
and Dr. Charles Jenkins. They both served
the Sandhills Region through their outstanding
commitment to developing outstanding
educational leaders.

By Dr. Thomas Benson

Serving as an educator and administrator of schools for twenty-six years has allowed me to experience the good, bad and the ugly. I have had the experience of serving as the principal of an alternative school, traditional middle and high school. I have also served as an assistant superintendent and also as a Federal Program Administrator at the North Carolina Department of Public Instruction, where I had the opportunity of coordinating the 2019 National Title I Distinguished School for North Carolina.

I completed a bachelor's degree at Wingate University, where I received an athletic scholarship for football; a Master's degree from Fayetteville State in Middle Grades Science; a master's degree from UNCP in School Administration, and a Doctoral degree from Wingate University.

I am a forward-thinking educator with expertise in maximizing the effectiveness of educational programs through strategic planning, curriculum, and program development. I began my career in education as a teacher assistant, then became a middle grades science teacher and school administrator. My first principalship was in Hoke County Schools as Principal of JW Turlington Alternative School. I later accepted principalships in Cumberland County Schools, where I served as Principal of Spring Lake Middle School and Westover High School. I also served as an Assistant Superintendent and lastly with the North Carolina Department of Public Instruction where I served as serve as a Federal Program Administrator for the North Carolina Department of Public Instruction with the Federal Program Monitoring and Support Division which supports approximately $514,000,000 in federal funds provided to districts and schools each year.

The primary role of our division was to provide grants administration, program monitoring, data collection and reporting, and to facilitate the necessary technical assistance to ensure not only compliance, but quality programs for students in the state of North Carolina. Compliance is the first step toward program quality; monitoring is the springboard to providing technical assistance. My secondary responsibility with the Division was to serve as the State Coordinator for Neglected or Delinquent grants administration. I provided program monitoring, data collection and reporting, and I facilitated the necessary technical assistance to ensure not only compliance to provide quality programs for students.

The Leandro Case

I currently serve as the Principal of Hoke High School, which is located in Raeford, North Carolina. Hoke County is known for the Leandro litigation which occurred in 1994, where five school systems sued the state of North Carolina seeking a declaration that the state of North Carolina had failed to meet its constitutional duties to provide an equal educational opportunity for all students and a court-imposed solution to correct the violation. Eventually the case was moved to a trial court where Superior Court Judge Howard E. Manning, Jr. presided over the hearing and issued four memoranda of decisions from October 2000 through May 2001, concluding that the State had failed to provide at-risk students with the opportunity to obtain a sound basic education and ordered the solution of providing pre-kindergarten to at-risk students (Ednc.org/leandro-litigation, 2022).

The State appealed and the Supreme Court agreed

to hear the appeal directly. In 2004, the Supreme Court, Justice Robert Orr, affirmed the trial court's order regarding at-risk students—with some modifications—and reversed regarding the prekindergarten, finding that the State should have been given the opportunity to propose a constitutional remedy before it was imposed by the court (Ednc. org/leandro-litigation, 2022).

Distinguished Schools High Progress and High Performance

This book will explore the demographics of Distinguished Schools and we will explore the details of the 2019 Distinguished Schools of North Carolina; the High Progress Schools and the High-Performance Schools. We will also explore the many different funding sources that are available for districts and schools to utilize to help their school's academic performance.

To understand High Progress and High Performance of the 2019 Distinguished Schools we will look at how high progress and high-performance schools are identified and the process used to identify those schools. We will also review each schools' methods and/or programs used to create best practices which have positively impacted the performance of those successful schools.

Finally, we will review the different funding sources

available to Title I Schools and how Federal funding can be used to enhance student learning opportunities for students.

We will first review the process used by the North Carolina Department of Public Instruction to identify High Progress and High-Performance Schools. Later we will identify the schools designated as high progress and high performance. Finally, we will review the summary of best practices used by those distinguished schools. The goal of this book is to provide a resource for acting principals and/ or future administrators that may be helpful to schools that are trying to improve student performance. Many of these practices and programs can be implemented, which in turn may effectively impact school performance.

The North Carolina National Title I Distinguished School Program recognizes exemplary Title I schools that maintain high standards and demonstrate outstanding best practices in:

- ❧ Teaching and learning aligned to the approved state curriculum,

- ❧ Research-based instructional practices,

- ❧ Creating opportunities for all students to achieve,

- ❧ Creating partnerships with parents, family, and the community,

- ❧ Creating sustained research-based professional development, and

- ❧ Creative innovation and modeling for other schools (NCDPI, 2021).

In 1996, North Carolina has recognized Distinguished Title I Schools through this program. Every year two North Carolina schools are recognized at the National level. Schools selected as North Carolina Title I Distinguished Schools are recognized in one or two categories. Schools in the Sustained High-Performance Category are recognized for showing a high (at least eighty percent) level of student proficiency in reading and mathematics and making Adequate Yearly Progress (AYP) for the most recent years. Schools in the Sustained High Growth Category are recognized for making significant progress in closing the achievement gap between student groups (NCDPI, 2021).

Once schools are selected based on their performance a committee of educators from across the state of North Carolina are selected to participate in scoring the portfolio packets that schools selected will complete and submit to North Carolina Department of Public Instruction by a designated timeframe.

The National Title I Distinguished Schools Portfolio consists of the following:

- Core/Assurance Page
- Parts A-E Narrative; and
- Partnering Agency/Organization Certification Pages.

The portfolio then breaks down each section of portfolio into categories with designated points for each area:

A. School Demographics (Ten Points),

B. Description of the Curriculum and Instructional Program, Initiative and Sustainability Plans (Thirty-five points),

C. Professional Development (Fifteen Points),

D. Collaboration, Family and Community Engagement (Twenty Points), and

E. Innovation and Model for Other Schools (Twenty Points) (National Title I Distinguished Schools North Carolina Portfolio, 2019).

During the 2019 Title I Distinguished Schools Portfolio submission the following schools were chosen by the scoring committee as the High Performance Schools the total amount of points a school could earn was three hundred:

- Riverbend Elementary (273),

- Pitt County Schools Early College High School (268),

- Hendersonville Elementary School (265),

- Union Elementary (Brunswick County) (259), and

- Bertie Early College High School of Agriscience & Biotechnology (208).

The High Progress Schools also could earn a total of three hundred points:

- West Elementary (Cleveland County) (280),

- D. F. Walker Elementary School (267),

- Union Elementary (Lincoln County) (241),

- Barringer Academic Center (CMS) (236), and

- Mountain View Elementary (224).

The scoring committee was able to trim the High-Performance Schools down to five schools and the High Progress Schools had five school sites. The highest score attainable was three hundred.

We will provide a breakdown of the demographics of each of the High-Performance Schools.

Riverbend Elementary School serves the largely underdeveloped, rural communities of Crabtree, Iron Duff, and Fine Creek. Riverbend serves a high number of unemployed, homeless, and disadvantaged families. The per capita income of $27,166 is about thirteen percent lower than the United States average. Haywood Counties median household income is approximately twenty-one percent lower than the U.S. median household income. The school's population of two hundred twenty-one students consists of ninety-five percent White, four percent Hispanic and less than one percent of both American Indian and Multiracial. Forty-two percent of student population receives free or reduced meals and nineteen-point eight percent are students with disabilities. The Academically Intellectually Gifted population is nine-point three percent. Sixty percent of students are in grades K-5 and receive targeted assistance through Title I.

Pitt County Schools Early College High School (PCSECHS) opened on August 10, 2015. The first year, PCSECHS employed four teachers, a counselor, a principal, an office manager, and a college liaison. The school had seventy-five students selected to attend the first year and each year seventy-five additional students were added.

The 2019 School year PCSECHS employed ten teachers, an instructional coach, counselor, clerical assistant, office manager, receptionist college liaison, and a principal. The student enrollment during the 2019 school year was three hundred fifteen students in grades nine through thirteen. Of those students, thirty-two percent were African American, thirty percent were Hispanic, thirty-three where Caucasian three percent were Multiracial, two percent were Asian. Of those students, sixty-nine percent were female, and thirty-one percent were male. Among the female students, thirty-three percent were African American, twenty-seven percent were Hispanic, thirty-three percent were Caucasian, four percent were Multiracial, and two percent were Asian. Of the male students, thirty percent were African American, thirty-five percent were Hispanic, thirty-two percent were Caucasian, one percent were Multiracial, and one percent were Asian.

Among the student population, eighty-six percent of the students are considered economically disadvantage, and eighty-eight percent are "First Generation" college-going students. First generation is defined as neither parent having obtained higher than an associate degree.

Hendersonville Elementary School is located in the rural town of Hendersonville, North Carolina in the Western part of the state. It is one of fifteen elementary schools in Henderson County. It is a K-5 school with an average student population of three hundred sixty-eight. HES is a non-districted year-round school. The school has three classes per grade level and two intensive intervention special needs classes serving primarily students with autism. Grades three through five are departmentalized. Hendersonville Elementary School is a targeted Title I school because thirty-seven percent of the student population was economically disadvantaged. The minority population of the school was seventeen percent comprised of point zero eight percent American Indian, point zero eight percent Asian, seven percent African American, six percent Hispanic and four percent Multiracial. The school has fifteen percent identified as Exceptional Children with Individualized Educational Plans (IEP's); nineteen percent were served in the Academically Intellectually Gifted program. The school has fourteen percent of K-2 students served by a Title I Literacy Intervention Program.

Union Elementary is located in Shallotte, North Carolina, and the school serves five hundred seventy-five students in grades K-5 in Southern Brunswick County, between Wilmington, NC and Myrtle Beach, South Carolina. In 1950, Union Elementary was an African American High School, and the school evolved into a thriving elementary school. The demographics of the school changed over the years creating a more diverse population where sixteen percent of the students were Hispanic, thirteen percent were African American, five percent were Multiracial, two percent were

Asian American Indian, and the remaining sixty-four percent were White. The English as a Second Language students are comprised of nine percent while the exceptional population grew to twelve percent. The biggest development was the growing number of free/reduced lunch percentage which was fifty-seven percent. The biggest challenge Union Elementary faces is the transiency of their students. The school has more students living in poverty, with grandparents or multiple families living together due to socio-economic issues, as well as hurricane damages over the years has drastically impacted this school.

Bertie Early College High School of Agriscience and Biotechnology is one of North Carolina's cooperative innovative high schools that is housed in one of the districts historic school buildings in the district. BECHS is located in Bertie County, Windsor, North Carolina. The school has one hundred eighty-one students in grades 9-13 and nineteen faculty and staff members. The school is made ups of sixty-six percent African American, twenty-nine percent White, and five percent Hispanic/Other. The student population varies from exceptional children to first generation students.

We will now review the High Progress Schools demographic data of each school recognized.

West Elementary School is a school-wide Title I school located in the heart of Kings Mountain, North Carolina, and positioned in Cleveland County. The school has three hundred thirty-two students enrolled in the pre-kindergarten through fourth grade. The student population consist of sixty-two percent Caucasian, twenty-four percent African American, six percent Hispanic, seven percent Multiracial. Students are served in a variety of programs designed to enhance and support core instruction for all learners. Nine percent of students are identified through the exceptional children's program, eight percent of students are identified as academically gifted, three percent are served through English Learners Program, and eighteen percent were identified as Tier II through the Multi-Tiered System of Support framework, twelve percent were identified as Tier III through the MTSS Framework, ten percent were eligible under section 504. Fifty-six-point six percent of students receive free or reduced lunch and are considered economically disadvantaged. Thirty-six percent of the students receive federal food assistance through the North Carolina Food Stamp program.

D. F. Walker Elementary School is located in Edenton, North Carolina. D. F. Walker Elementary has four hundred thirty-five students in grades three, four and five. The school is a Title I school with three hundred thirteen (72%) students receiving free or reduced lunch. The student body consists of one hundred ninety-six students (45%) African American, one hundred thirty-one (30%) Caucasian, forty-three (10%) Hispanic, and twenty-six (6%) Multiracial. The school also serves students in the academically and intellectually gifted, students with disabilities, economically disadvantaged, and English Language Learners. Students are identified for interventions, enrichment, programs, and initiatives based on data collection, disaggregation, analysis, and reporting provides data that highlights targeted instruction for every student.

Union Elementary School is located in Vale, North Carolina and serves two hundred eighty-two students (PreK-5th grade) students, where forty-eight percent participate in the National School Lunch Program. Union Elementary School is located in the rural area of Western Lincoln County. The population consists of one hundred thirty-seven males, one hundred forty-five females, fifteen Hispanic students, three African American students, twenty multiracial students, and two hundred forty-four Caucasian students. Union Elementary school serves an academically diverse student population which consists of twenty-three percent of students with disabilities, three percent of students are academically gifted, five percent of students are English Language Learners, and fifteen percent of students are served in the Title I reading program.

Barringer Academic Center School is located in Charlotte, North Carolina, and has five hundred students with the largest demographic being African

American students. The school is comprised of fifty-one-point six percent of African American students, with twenty-five point four percent Asian, eleven point two percent White, ten percent Hispanic, one point two percent Multiracial, and point two percent American Indian.

Forty percent of students come to the school from South Charlotte for the Gifted Magnet Program. The families come from a more affluent area of Charlotte including Matthews, Lake Wylie, and Ballantyne. Approximately sixty percent of students come from the West Boulevard Corridor. Nine percent of students are considered students with disabilities, twenty-seven percent considered Academically-Intellectually Gifted, two percent considered as McKinney-Vento and six-point six percent are considered English Language Learners.

Mountain View Elementary School is located in Hickory, North Carolina, serving seven hundred thirty students pre-K through 6th grade. Thirty-nine percent of students participate in the National School Lunch Program. The school is located in the rural area of Southwestern Catawba County. The population consists of three hundred eighty-one males, three hundred forty-nine females, five hundred thirty-nine Caucasian students, thirty-eight African American students, forty-eight Hispanic students, forty-two Asian students, sixty-two Multiracial students and one Native Hawaiian student. The school has one hundred two students with disabilities, twenty-seven English Language Learners, and one hundred thirty-three students receive research-based interventions in reading and/or math by an academic facilitator.

Best Practices

We will now explore the best practices for each of the High Performance and High Progress Schools. RiverBend Elementary creates an individual plan based on the needs of each student, data is collected and analyzed from sources like CLI Engage, mClass assessments and progress monitoring, state, and local benchmark data, reading assessments (Teachers College, Scholastic Reading Inventory, Wilson Assessment for Decoding and Encoding, etc.), ongoing formative assessments, teacher observations and student screenings. Specific data are recorded and updated frequently throughout the year to provide teachers with the opportunity to provide differentiation and interventions that change based on student needs. The school also has strategic vertical and horizontal data conversations among teachers, support staff and administrators to focus on the alignment with curriculum.

Teachers also use qualitative and quantitative data to assess data for creating flexible learning groups in their classrooms. Students may be identified based on their need for intensive enrichment or support from teachers, specialist, assistants, or volunteers.

Pitt County Schools Early College High School ensures that if a student's average drops below eighty percent in their high school work, they are required to attend afterschool tutoring in at least one of their areas of weakness until they have mastered this information. If a student performs poorly on an assessment, they are required to reflect on their learning and to improve through test revisions. Also, if a student's average drops below eighty percent in college coursework, they are required to access tutoring and support services through Pitt Community College via the Tutorial and Academic Success Center (TASC) and/or TRIO: Educational Opportunity Center which serves a student at the school.

Hendersonville Elementary School has implemented strategies such as STEM and Problem/project-based learning (PBL) to support instructional goals across all subject areas. The STEM activities help students make connections and transfer information between subjects. The school also holds STEM events where students can showcase their learning and STEM Products. Students are given STEM challenges, which help them apply their knowledge and practice perseverance. The school also created a school wide focus on growth mindset, and they implemented Stephen R. Covey's The 7 Habits of Happy Kids. Also, the master schedule includes time for character building lessons.

Union Elementary (Brunswick County) focused on merging the Jan Richardson Guided Reading framework with the other components of Daily Five (Vocabulary, Word Work, Phonics, and Fluency). This provided a more focused literacy block in all grade levels, and it also provided a more consistent and rigorous instructional approach. The school focused on writing where they used the Empowering Writing Program to teach students how to write narrative and opinion pieces, informational texts, and constructed responses. Union Elementary School also began the process of becoming a 1:1 initiative in technology, providing blended learning experiences for students. Teachers also researched websites, applications, and programs (Flocabulary, Reading A to Z, Storyworks, EPIC!, Readworks, NewsELA) to support instruction and allow students to apply digital learning competencies.

Bertie Early College High School of Agriscience and Biotechnology focused on powerful teaching and learning strategies to provide differentiated instruction for all types of learners. Teachers also incorporated reading and writing and speaking across the curriculum. The school also focused on ACT Prep, Character Education/Emotional Intelligence training, and Financial Literacy and built-in remediation for EOC's was implemented daily.

The High Progress schools focused on different instructional strategies to ensure that progress for all students was continuous and effective. West Elementary (Cleveland County) focused on several practices.

Utilization of the North Carolina Multi-Tiered System of Support where core instruction is evaluated and monitored for all students at the Tier I level. Students needing additional support are offered a variety of interventions at Tier II and Tier III levels. Benchmarking data is gathered three times per year to determine a child's ability to apply foundational literacy and mathematical skills. In the area of literacy, the school focused on the utilization of mClass—Amplify, which is twoprong assessment tool. DIBELs (Dynamic Indicator of Beginning Early Literacy Skills Assessment) is an early intervention assessment tool that assesses foundational reading skills based on a grade level progression guide and mClass Reading 3-D Assessment data is used to determine applicable reading skills. In turn, the school split their students into homogenous groups for guided reading based on their TRC (Text to Reading Comprehension) levels.

CBMs (Curriculum-Based Measures) are utilized to measure basic understanding of number sense in mathematics. This tool allows teachers to evaluate student mathematics skill acquisition and plan interventions based on data.

A focus on SEL (Social-Emotional Learning) time occurs twenty to thirty minutes a day where the classroom teacher focuses on Second Step Program to integrate Social-Emotional Learning, Bullying Prevention, and Child Protection to create a cohesive foundation for a safe and supportive learning environment.

Science and Social Studies are taught with the focus on hands-on and experimental learning approaches. Materials such as Scholastic News, Discovery Magazines, Social Studies Weekly, Science Weekly, and Discovery Education Websites are used to teach content standards in conjunction with informational reading standards.

D. F. Walker Elementary School focuses on providing all students three tiers of high-quality instructional support. Ninety-minute blocks where core instruction is differentiated and tightly aligned to content standards. They use research-based components of balanced literacy, evidence-based math practices and a strong focus on Tiered vocabulary using the strategies of Marzano. Core instructional resources aligned to the North Carolina Standards include Wonders Reading, Engage NY Math with NC Tools for Teachers, and StemScopes Science.

Targeted, small group instruction, focused on individual student needs, provides scaffolding, and reteach methods such as Leveled Literacy Intervention and i-Ready. Adaptive digital platforms such as Freckle and Moby Max, as well as mClass, the Florida Center for Reading and Intervention Central are used to provide intensive interventions.

Union Elementary School (Lincoln County Schools) strive to meet the social, emotional, and academic needs of each individual student by providing a safe and nurturing environment. "Positive Behavior Interventions Supports" they promote positive behavior daily. The students start each day in a positive environment and together they pledge that they will O—Own our own actions, W—work hard to succeed, L—Lead with kindness, and S—

show respect (OWLS). Union Elementary School combines their character education program with Kiwanis Terrific Kids to promote and instill lifelong values. These activities are introduced monthly through classroom guidance lessons and are reinforced and supported throughout the entire school.

The school has focused on a balanced literacy approach to ensure that the student needs are met around English Language Arts. They have used several programs: Saxon Phonics, Leveled Readers, Pioneer Valley Literacy Footprints, RAZ Kids, Fountas and Pinnell Shared Reading Kits and Interactive Read Aloud. Also, they have used NC Ready Reading, Scholastic News, and novel studies. NC Ready Math is provided for all K-5 teachers, and teachers continue to use teacher created material, hands-on manipulatives, real world application through concrete, representational and abstract teaching approach. Math interventions are provided through research-based interventions and utilizing the Do the Math and Number World Programs.

Barringer Academic Center utilizes the framework

for delivering Core or Tier I instruction is provided through planning that emphasizes a commitment to individual learning via differentiation, inclusion, and personalized learning, all of which are research based best practices. Barringer Academic Center provides a Learning Immersion Program, which is available for K-5 students. The program is built on the premise that nurturing students higher level thinking and providing them multiple opportunities to demonstrate their intelligence will lead them to gifted certification.

Mountain View Elementary School provides all students that are not on grade level, will receive interventions based on data collected from iStation and Aimsweb Assessments, local benchmark assessments and teacher observations. To meet grade level expectations, identified students are placed in the tier process. Teachers use the Reading, Math, and Behavior Protocol created by the district to address essential components of these areas. The Academic Facilitator serves students encountering difficulty each day for additional reading support in grades K-6.

For math, teachers use the NC Early Numeracy Skill Indicators, NC Check-ins, SchoolNet and local benchmark assessments to gather student understanding in math. Math interventions are used to drill down to the skills of each student.

In the area of reading the school has placed an emphasis on Letterland, Language, and Title I reading programs, guided reading instruction, vocabulary enrichment higher order and written response across all grade levels. Letterland phonics is used in grades preK through 2 and has been implemented into 3rd grade to help close the achievement gap. Academic Facilitator and tutors use data to pull small groups daily to build on strengths and to teach effective reading strategies. Guided reading instruction takes place throughout the school and differentiated leveled texts are used in small groups. Literacy exercises address standards and produce authentic engagement.

In conclusion, visiting many of these schools during the site visits allowed myself and my team to get a feel for the culture and many of these schools have focused on creating and sustaining a positive culture built on relationships with students, teachers, parents, and all stakeholders.

Funding Sources

The following funding sources may be used to support your initiatives for school improvement:

- ℂ **Title I:**

    The local educational agency (LEA) has the flexibility to use Title I funds for various activities that would enhance the academic achievement of at-risk children served under Title I funds, these activities must either be authorized in the Elementary and Secondary Education Act (ESEA) or meet the general standards and prohibitions established in Office of Management and Budget (OMB) (Kesslar, 2017)

- ℂ **Title II:**

    SEC. 2001. 20 U.S.C. 6601, PURPOSE.

The purpose of this title is to provide grants to State educational agencies and subgrants to local educational agencies to—

1. increase student achievement consistent with the challenging State academic standards,

2. improve the quality and effectiveness of teachers, principals, and other school leaders,

3. increase the number of teachers, principals, and other School leaders who are effective in improving student academic Achievement in schools, and

4. Provide low-income and minority students greater access to effective teachers, principals, and other school leaders (ESEA, 2021).

ಞ **Title III:**

SEC. 3102. 20 U.S.C. 6812: PURPOSES. The purposes of this part are—(1) to help ensure that English learners, including immigrant children and youth, attain English proficiency and develop high levels of academic achievement in English; (2) to assist all English learners, including immigrant children and youth, to achieve at high levels in academic subjects so that all English learners can meet the same challenging State academic standards that all children are expected to meet; (3) to assist teachers (including preschool teachers), principals and other school leaders, State educational agencies, local educational agencies, and schools in establishing, implementing, and sustaining effective language instruction educational programs designed to assist in teaching English learners, including immigrant children and youth; (4) to assist teachers (including preschool teachers), principals and other school leaders, State educational agencies, and local educational agencies to develop and enhance their capacity to provide effective instructional programs designed to prepare English learners, including immigrant children and youth, to enter all-English instructional settings. (5) to promote parental, family, and community participation in language instruction educational programs for the parents, families, and communities of English learners (ESEA, 2021).

‰ Title IV:

The purpose of this subpart is to improve students' academic achievement by increasing the capacity of States, local educational agencies, schools, and local communities to—(1) provide all students with access to a well-rounded education; (2) improve school conditions for student learning; and (3) in order to improve the academic achievement and digital literacy of all students (ESEA, 2021).

‰ Neglected or Delinquent Funds

PURPOSE.—It is the purpose of this part—(1) to improve educational services for children and youth in local, tribal, and State institutions for neglected or delinquent children and youth so that such children and youth have the opportunity to meet the same challenging State academic standards that all children in the State are expected to meet. (2) to provide such children and youth with the services needed to make a successful transition from institutionalization to further schooling or employment; and (3) to prevent at-risk youth from dropping out of school, and to provide dropouts, and children and youth returning from correctional facilities or institutions for neglected or delinquent children and youth, with a support system to ensure their continued education and the involvement of their families and communities. (b) PROGRAM AUTHORIZED.—In order to carry out the purpose of this part and from amounts appropriated under section 1002 (d), the Secretary shall make grants to State educational agencies to enable such agencies to award subgrants to State agencies and local educational agencies to establish or improve programs of education for neglected, delinquent, or at-risk children and youth (ESEA, 2021).

Conclusion

As we now battle to move schools back to normal, we must be willing to look back on many of the practices that made profound impacts on student achievement within the state of North Carolina. The pandemic has made it a challenge for educators to feel comfortable returning to schools but with our educational leaders we must be more inventive with our methods and consider programs that enhance social/emotional learning such as:

- Responsive Classrooms

- Second Step

- Conscious Discipline

- The 4 Rs

- Newsela SEL

In the summary section of this book, you will find a breakdown of the most relevant aspects of the best practices utilized by the High-Performance Schools and the High Progress Schools.

2019 Distinguished Schools Best Practices

(Highest possible points earned: 300)

School	Best Practice
Riverbend Elementary (273) High Performance	• Literacy Block of at least 120 minutes, read aloud, shared, guided and independent Reading. • Small Group Reading, Individual reading goals. • Balanced Literacy Approach for all students. • Reading and writing workshops for teachers; and increased rigor within Balanced Literacy. • Teachers track students' fluency using Teachers college benchmarks for oral reading rates, A to Z Fluency, or Read Naturally. • Implemented new Tools 4 NC Teachers and continued with *Investigations.* • PD: Comprehension Toolkit, STEM-Scopes, and *Investigations.* • Lucy Calkins Reading Workshop.

Pitt County Schools Early College High School (Winner) (268) High Performance	• Powerschool and finance workshops; Faculty Senate, Power Standards Development; Monthly Counselor Meetings, Principal Meetings; Instructional Coaches Meeting; Learning Focused Lesson Planning and Higher Order Thinking, Thinking Maps. • Ron Clark Academy; AVID professional development. • Buck Institute: Project Based learning.
Hendersonville Elementary School (265) High Performance	• Integrated writing throughout all subject areas, engage students in error analysis, preview, and scaffold, teach vocabulary explicitly, and utilize collaborative pairs. • Students are taught to question and develop higher order thinking skills as they dive into standards and STEM tasks. • Students receive differentiated instruction during core blocks and Cubcat time, which is an extra period during the day where students receive additional intervention/extension opportunities.

Union elementary (Brunswick) (259) High Performance	• Balanced Literacy Framework • Jan Richardson Guided Reading Framework with other components of Daily Five (Vocabulary, Word Work, Phonics, and Fluency). • Empowering Writing Program: used to teach students how to write narrative and opinion pieces, informational texts, and constructed responses. • Guided Math Instruction: Teachers provided small group/hands-on approach which allowed teachers to teach and assess mastery of concepts, and clear up misconceptions.
Bertie Early College High School (208) High Performance	• Powerful teaching and learning strategies are differentiated to accommodate the various learning styles of each student. • Teachers incorporate reading and writing and speaking across the curriculum. • ACT Prep, Character Ed/Emotional Intelligence training, and Financial Literacy.

West Elementary (280) High Progress	<ul><li>Multi-Tiered System of Support with layered interventions for students.</li><li>CBM (Curriculum Based Measures): utilized to measure basic understanding of number sense in mathematics for all students.</li><li>SEL (Social-Emotional Learning) Teachers utilize the Second Step Program to teach social skills instruction. The Second Step Program integrates social-emotional learning, bullying prevention, and child protection to form a cohesive foundation for a safe and supportive learning environment.</li><li>English Language Arts block is based on the Fountas and Pinnell balanced literacy framework. The model encompasses, literacy and informational text review through shared reading, guided reading, self-selected reading, read aloud, and vocabulary study.</li><li>Shared reading is taught in a whole group setting using grade-level literacy and informational texts with explicit teacher instruction of comprehension and decoding strategies.</li><li>Guided Reading is a time where teachers select text based on a student's instructional level to provide direct instruction during small flexible groups.</li><li>Students are exposed to above grade level texts during a teacher read aloud when teachers model monthly comprehension strategies and fluency for students.</li></ul>

<table>
<tr>
<td></td>
<td>

- LLI (Leveled Literacy Instruction) is prominently used in the primary grades to promote strong literacy skills and teachers in third and fourth grade utilize short reads and leveled texts as a way of promoting overall text comprehension that covers. All subject areas.

- The Comprehension Toolkit by Stephanie Harvey and Anne Goudvis is utilized in kindergarten through fourth grade as part of the balanced literacy framework. Each month teachers unveil a comprehension strategy that is utilized in whole and small group sessions to encourage rigor in reading and active participation with informational and fictional text selections.

- Math Program components used are Eureka math, motivation mathematics, Go Math, and IXL Math.

- Guided Math: is a time where teachers work with students to assess their understanding of math standards and assist with concept mastery.

</td>
</tr>
</table>

D. F. Walker Elementary School (Winner) (267) High Progress	• Balanced Literacy Focused on each student's level of ability. • DFW PD framework of three tiers: Whole School PD, Grade Level PLCs, and Optional Differentiated PLCs. Tier one: data driven research-based PD which creates a culture of continuous learning and implements an instructional continuum for students across the school. Tier two: staff attend weekly grade level PLCs where the research-based PD topic is continued with a more targeted approach for the specific needs of the grade level data. Tier three: the school offers weekly school-wide Optional Differentiated PLCs. The PD is differentiated by curriculum and/or skill level (beginning, intermediate, and advanced) to ensure that all individual staff are receiving the support they need. • Monday morning Music for students entering the cafeteria is a positive culture reinforcement tool. • Facebook live concept reaches all students, parents, and community members. • Leadership empowers teachers to lead based on skill level. • Principal's relationships and passion for High Expectations is contagious.

Barringer Academic Center (236) **High Progress**	• Academic Initiatives: AVID or B3 (Body, Brain, and Behavior), emotional initiatives such as Chess, Chorus, Let Me Run and Girls on the Run.
Mountain View Elementary (224) **High Progress**	• Letterland phonics programs in grades Pre-K, 2 and have implemented into 3rd grade to help close the achievement gap. • Guided Reading instruction takes place throughout the school and differentiated leveled texts are used in small groups.

References:

Elementary and Secondary Education Act of 1965. http://www2.ed.gov. 2021

Kesslar, T. (2017). *Can Title I Pay for This? A guide to determining Allowable Cost.* FL.

McColl, A. (2020). *Everything you need to know about Leandro Litigation.* http://www.ednc.org/leandro.Litigation/

NCDPI (2021). Title I Distinguished Schools. http://www.dpi.nc.gov.2021

High Performance School of 2019

Pitt Early College High School

High Progress School of 2019

D. F. Walker Elementary School

About the Author

Dr. Thomas Benson III grew up in the small town of Lyman, South Carolina, in the seventies, spending his childhood years on his aunts' farm. He has received a master's degree from both Fayetteville State University and The University of North Carolina at Pembroke, followed by a doctoral degree from Wingate University. Dr. Benson is a dynamic educator of many years and mentors' young adults through establishing meaningful relationships and sharing his life experiences. He currently lives in Raeford, North Carolina, with his wife, son, and daughter.